THE RAPE KIT
TERRI WITEK

The Rape Kit
© 2018 Terri Witek

Cover image, "Reliquaries #1 (for Terri)" by Cyriaco Lopes
Design by Lucianna Chixaro Ramos

Library of Congress Cataloging-in-Publication Data

Names: Witek, Terri, 1952- author.
Title: The rape kit / Terri Witek.
Description: Northampton : Slope Editions, 2018.
Identifiers: LCCN 2018001515 | ISBN 9780988522176 (pbk.)
Classification: LCC PS3623.I86 A6 2018 | DDC 811/.6--dc23
LC record available at https://lccn.loc.gov/2018001515

Slope Editions, created by Ethan Paquin & Christopher Janke in 2001, works toward the goal of presenting readers with a fine and eclectic array of poetry. Each year, we release one to two well-chosen & stylistically diverse softcover, perfect-bound books & chapbooks that defy convention & categorization. Among those who have taken note of our work are Publishers Weekly, Poets & Writers, PN Review, & other publications across the world. Our titles are distributed to the trade by SPD & Baker & Taylor. Slope Editions is part of Slope Publishing Inc., a registered non-profit literary and educational organization with 501(c)(3) status.

TABLE OF CONTENTS

2. WHERE THE LOST THINGS GO

3. LIES DOWN WITH

4. LET'S TRY THIS AGAIN: HOW DID YOU TRAVEL?

INTRODUCTION
BY DAWN LUNDY MARTIN

I have long used writing about rape as an example for the unsayable. How does one say it: "rape," and have it resonate with the deficit experience of rape? How does one put language to the trauma of the experience without reducing it, without captioning it alongside the experience like some lone language predicated on our cultural limitations that both accept and exceptionalize this kind of violation? What Terri Witek has done in her visceral and haptic book of poems, The Rape Kit, is create a new language for breaking open the trauma of sexual violation.

Witek takes us inside of the legislation of bodies and cracks open the apparatuses around rape—around the regulation and smashing down of persons who are violated within a gendered regime that seeks to remain in power. In doing this, she reveals a familiar procedural performance of care, an undergirding work that professes a legislative desire for justice while supporting a reversal of victimhood. We want to help you, says the police. We don't believe you, is the underscore. This procedural performance of care, in Witek's rendering, is stripped of any resemblance to actual care. It becomes simply procedure—rote mechanizations in a pretend feeling world, tight and bottled inside of the bureaucracies that create the world.

Poetry often offers a way of new thinking about battered topics. Witek's poetry offers, in addition, new possibilities for poetry itself. I want to gather some of this newness here in microcosm. Her attention is sometimes directly on the thing at stake: "raped by a stranger as my children slept." Sometimes a radical turning away:

sideways-rushing sapphirine

where's Africa?

3 Solo birds

in 8 hours.

In the curiosity of this latter moment, seemingly private, also a breaking. The dotted line drawn down the page. The drawing of a key. That language is sometimes impossible. That we look away to continents and birds and hours. The border line in hyphenate. The border between before and after. That the utterances are not certain, that they skirt and stretch and fall away entirely is what gets us closer to the state of being incurred in the context under the scope here. Terri Witek brings us to the fractured state. She is like a sculptor refusing to elevate the materials but instead the underneath—the rooms that must be drawn. Witek flips the script—becomes master inside of the experience, and she brings us in too.

What must be drawn is what cannot be said. I think of M. NourbeSe Phllip and her phenomenal ZONG!, how it howls and limps breaking open its word store to show us the slaves thrown overboard the slave ship, giving them the voice they were denied. I think of think of the fake legal mechanisms at work that deny them humanity. Witek, too, shows us the under belly—but in her case the rape ship. She cascades a new language for the prison language of now. Terrance Hayes takes it up, conceptually, in his How to Be Drawn. So does Theresa Hak Kyung Cha in her time. We live in a time where women of all races, all classes and subject positions in the United-States-peril, are stepping into their now of speech, to say, like, Philip, we are human.

What The Rape Kit does with such ranging precision is expose the apparatus, which is the tenacious glue that holds us all in a stupid place. Terri Witek has changed my mind. Rape is not an unsayable experience. Its trauma might be beyond ordinary speech. But it is not beyond poetry. Rope or no rope.

1
THE RAPE KIT

Ladies and Gentlemen: In a few moments, several objects will appear in the line-up area. You will be able to see them, but they will not be able to see you. Each will be asked to do certain things, such as turning, speaking, etc.

When the entire line has completed this process, we will ask whether anyone desires one or more objects to repeat itself. If you do, please write your request on a card we will give you, raise your hand and an officer will take your card. In the event one object is asked to repeat a word or action, we will ask the entire line to repeat it.

Please do not talk with each other at any time. Communicate only with the officer, and then do so only in writing. When the line-up is completed, please fill out the card we have given you and hand it to the officer whether you have made an identification or not. If you cannot identify an object, please so indicate. If you can, mark the card with its numerical place in the line.

You are under no obligation to discuss this case or your identification with anyone, but you may do so if you wish.

Can You Take Us Thru What Happened?

another elegiac door with its animal

#

faulty the fire

#

who was netted at his side in unlucky pelt

#

swallowed the night next entered

#

tape condom flashlight rope

raped by a stranger as my children slept

History of the U.S. (Mary Rowlandson *and* **Michael Jackson**)

But out we must go, the fire increasing and coming along behind us, roaring **as we danced**, and the *moments* gaping before us with guns, spears, and hatchets to devour us. No sooner were we out of the house, but my brother-in-law (being before wounded in or near the throat) fell down dead, whereat the hour scornfully shouted, and hallowed, and was presently upon him, stripping off his clothes. The bullets lying thick **on the floor**, one went through my side, and the same (as would seem) through the bowels and hand of my dear child in my arms. Thus were we butchered by those merciless *times*, standing amazed, with the blood running down. Then *years* **in the round** laid hold of us, pulling me one way, and the children another, and said, "Come go along with us"—I told them they would kill me: they answered, if I were willing to go along with them, they would not hurt me.

Crime Scene w/ LANDSCAPE*

sobs sobbing pounding on door barking in distance
TV turns on metal clangs MOUNTAIN clears throat
door slams GROANING chuckles sighs sighs

sniffles groaning alarm blares panting sighs
thunder rumbles deep breaths bird calling shivering
PLANETREE door closes CICADA CICADA

shivers singsong voice normal voice
spits sniffs spits sighs sniffs
buzzer HE'S SICK clicking sighs handcuffs clicking

sighs sighs sighs MY HUSBAND
chuckles sighs voice breaking receiver thuds
handcuffs clicking grunts scream in distance

BLUE CHAIR breathing heavily groans
buckle clinks whispering NO MONEY zipper opens

*Sound effect subtitles.
Season 3, The Killing

18

Interlude in Which She Tried to Escape into a Tree

fold

fold

Dryad Sound Booth

the rigging
she expects
the pitch
(sighs)
that sax
that tenor
(grunts)
not wedded to
the historical
(clinking)
to the lost
archive of trees
(sighs)
that theater
(door opens)
of one
(hiss)
rendering
(s)
(

What Happened When Knife Entered Tree

It skipped deeper.
Gone: shame's sunset flak-jacket.

////

Just one more looped scratch.
After the next sap storm (but trees

lead slower lives so who knows?)
a name wobbled then walked.

It tried a new little sound
and the forest replied.

No, that was the knife getting smarter,
poking around like a flashlight.

Flashlight

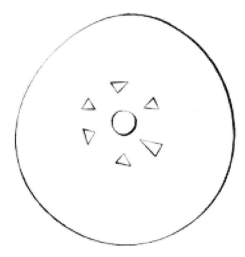

Can You Walk Us Thru It?

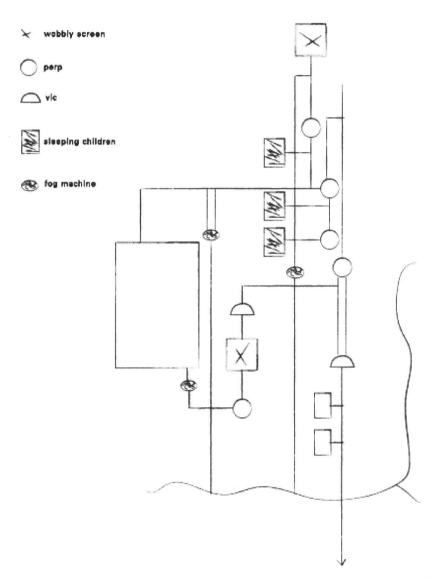

groans

straining

grunts

grunting

coughs

radio chatter

laughter

indistinct talking

metal grinds

panting

creaking

door opens, closes

sighs

clears throat

door closes

indistinct talking

sighs

sniffs

car horn honks in distance

sighs

phone beeps

door opens

sniffles

sniffles

crying

crying

sniffles

sniffles

camera shutter clicking

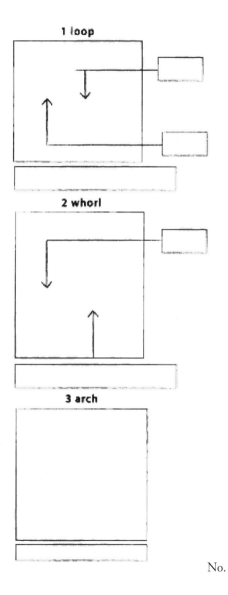

Now Tell Us About the Weapon

Gunbarrel

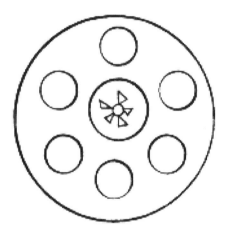

How many temples in the river city of _____?
At which degrees do _____ jar their pollen?

The termites who slipped in with her
are laughing their little legs off.

crow cawing

voice breaking

indistinct
conversations

indistinct
conversations

sighs

sighs

cellphone ringing

sighs

cellphone beeps

radio chatter

dog barks in distance

sighs

breathes deeply

sighs

gulls squawking

indistinct
conversations

dialing cellphone

beeps

laughs

thud

knock on door

knock on door

clattering

zipper closes

paper rustles

door opens

crying

ice cream truck plays

sprinkler spraying

sighs

engine turns over

gulls squawking

thud

scoffs

door closes

sighs

cellphone beeps

footsteps approach

clicks tongue

exhales sharply

sighs

clicks tongue

voice breaking

sighs

sighs

sighs

radio chatter

insects chirping

tires squeal

car horn blares

gasps

retching and coughing

breathing deeply

loon calling

breathes deeply

loon calling

gun cocks

doorknob rattles

clatter

siren in distance

gunshot

inhales sharply

slowly groans

groaning

breathes shakily

gasping

gunshot

insects chirping

The consent **-Oh-** which is implied in every agreement is excluded 1. by error in the essentials of the contract **-did I offend it-** as if Paul, in the city of Philadelphia, buy the horse of Peter, which is in Boston, and promise to pay 100 dollars for him, the horse at the time of the sale, unknown to either ***Didn't want me*** party being dead. This decision is founded on the rule that he who consents ***to tell it the truth*** through error does not consent at all; non consentiunt qui errant. 2. Consent is excluded by the duress of the party making the agreement 3. Consent is never given so as to bind **-Daisy-** the parties when it is obtained by fraud. 4. It cannot be given by a person who has no **-Daisy-** understanding, as an idiot, nor by one who, though possessed of understanding, is not in law capable of making **-offend it-** a Contract, as *a feme Couvert.*

All Quiet at 2AM

it's over

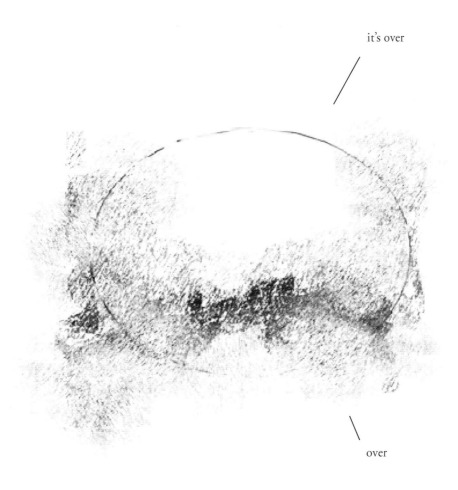

over

.........we operate under the premise that whenever human beings interact with any inanimate or animate object, something is either taken away or left behind.

Dr. Larry (the Jet) Jetmore
Goals for Searching the Crime Scene

UH-OH

Like anyone, he's lost his keys.

grid searching

advance on the strip method searchers
complete the strip method and double
back across the area being searched

Quizlet's Crime Search Methods

cicada cicada cicada cicada cicada cicada cicada cicada cicada cicada cicada cicada cicada cicada cicada cicada cicada cicada cicada **...pull** cicada cicada cicada cicada cicada cicada cicada cicada cicada cicada cicada cicada **the little river asid**e cicada cicada cicada cicada cicada cicada cicada cicada cicada cicada cicada cicada cicada one gold bead cicada cicada cicada cicada cicada cicada cicada cicada cicada cicada **a crystal-headed pin** cicada **amphorae w/ elliptical mouths** cicada **no goats** cicada cicada cicada cicada cicada cicada cicada cicada cicada cicada cicada **no dogs** cicada **wings open above** cicada **and below the body** cicada

Flashlight

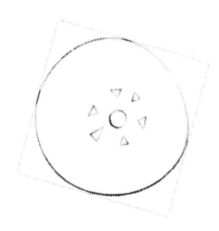

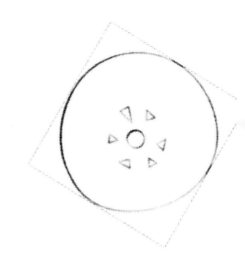

sliver

silver

2 Years Later

telephone thuds
ringing continues
ringing continues

His Van was Stopped for Erratic Driving

tape	**condom**	**flashlight**	**rope**
tap	conundrum	flesh loot	ripe
tip	cum hum	flush late	reap
type	candy man	fake clit	rip
trap	can do man	fate click	rape

Lordy, the Fingerprints Match

applause

reporters shouting indistinctly

sighs

ringing

phone closes

crying

sighs

sighs

door rattles open

groans

sighs

sighs

gate rattles shut

sighs

sniffles

sniffs

BOTH LAUGHING

chuckles

chuckles

chuckles

exhales sharply

chuckles

key rattles in lock

door closes

sighs

sighs

sighs

sighs

sighs

sighs

sobbing

More Years On

q. what's a little late?
    a. always

q. dressed for war, how do we dance?
    a. partition our garments
    a. marry the dead

History of the US (Tree Removal and **Cognitive Interview Technique**)

there goes the chain won't make it hey Jo Jo **can you say** don't need it watch your head Papi you the fork hey the big one don't bother come on grab don't fuss the posture pull up uh, oh, I need more of that flip the guy in here we go steady can't figure **what happened** Randall the little tree right there wait a minute I gotta don't break big dead hey hey gotta swing it hold it whooo hey hey no ties back **backwards** to me babe hey I need it hey

Drowse-making heat.

Lay some sweet lines on me, baby.
Yes sir, we swallowed it hook, line and sinker.

Most detectives interrupted responses to open-ended questions after 7.5 seconds. Not one of the interviews studied had a victim that was allowed to complete an uninterrupted response.

MCSA Victim Interviews

Because   I hadn't   illed a   ybody, I   idn't cu   anybod   , I didn't   tab any   ody,
som   how I di   n't see i   as that   ad. So I h   d this p   le of cr   p in
my ba   kgroun   and I sp   ay pain   ed itan   I put th   se flow
rs on it   nd I tri   d to make   t seem l   ke it wa   someth   ng diff
rent tha   it was. B   t as I beg   n to hon   stly lo   k at the   hings
I   ave don   , it was a r   al chal   enge to   e to hon   stly ac   ept
that.   feel li   e I've do   e as muc   as a per   on can d   to be re
ponsib   e.

They also tend to spontaneously justify the few things that they are telling you, even though you've not asked them any why **do you still** questions. It's as if they're trying to get you to believe them. There are also vocal **wear** indicators. A person who is lying will often start out answering a question slowly and then speed up. Probably they start out slow because they're trying to think of what their answer should be, but then as they realize they're not being forthcomin**G** or don't appear to be, they'l**L** speed up **O**nce they'**VE** got their **S**tory together.

elastic waistband

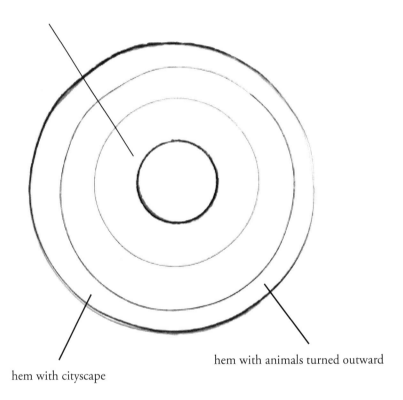

hem with cityscape

hem with animals turned outward

History of the US (Dan Turner, father of rapist/swimmer Brock, and **the nymph Arethusa**)

You can see this in his face the way **wherever I moved my foot** he walks, his weakened voice, his lack of appetite. Brock always enjoyed certain types of food and is a very good cook himself. I was always excited to buy him **a pool gathered**, a big ribeye steak to grill or to get his favorite snack for him. I had to make sure to hide some of my pretzels or chips **and faster than I can now** because I knew they wouldn't be around long after Brock walked in from a long swim practice. Now he barely consumes any food and eats only to exist. These verdicts have broken and shattered him and our family in so many ways. His life **tell the tale** will never be the one that he dreamed about and worked so hard to achieve. That is a steep price to pay for 20 minutes of action **I turned to water** out of his 20 plus years of life.

2
WHERE ALL THE LOST THINGS GO

EVIDENCE

(TO BE OPENED BY AUTHORIZED PERSONNEL ONLY)

--- NOTE ---
A) DO NOT USE THIS BAG FOR ANY EVIDENCE THAT HAS WET/DAMP BODY FLUIDS ON IT.
B) TO SEAL BAG, PEEL OFF RELEASE LINER, THEN SEAL BAG BY PRESSING DOWN ON GLUE LINE.

CASE NUMBER: _____

DESCRIPTION OF ENCLOSED EVIDENCE: _____

SUBMITTING AGENCY: _____

TELEPHONE NUMBER: _____

EVIDENCE RECORDED BY: _____
(PRINT NAME)

VICTIM'S FULL NAME: _____

SUSPECT'S FULL NAME: _____

EVIDENCE BAG SEALED BY: _____
(PRINT NAME)

_____
(SIGNATURE)

DATE SEALED: _____ TIME SEALED: _____ AM PM

History of the US (Jane Bennett and **the Green Hills Rapist**)

Objects are not inert mass we control but have their own often slower time,
ecosystems, nexuses of meaning--they are assemblages-this word **I** is a collusion
of screen, fingerprint, bacteria (6 different kinds at work on the bend of your arm),
a factory, a storm that **raped them** brought the system down. Even if it is **basically**
functional--I shaped to your hand, objects have their own tangled lives. They too
are **terrorized them** earthlings.

Why We Lie Down with Readymades

(golden shovel)

Habit (any old):
we twin a fetishized real
and bed down in cool
ilex. We
seem built for this myth, what's left
post breezy old-school
bravura-now we
bait, via peepshow and breeze lurk,
a strange (and late)
hour. So what if we
strip lightning from strike?
Some fool will stup us straight
later. Does naked we
still try to make moons sing?
Test it yourself: sin
variegatedly but ohsoswe
eetly within.
When gravity's g's begin,
smack through to a new we
and be-jazz
us, Lordy. Another wet June.
How not alone we
dead dying die
as all the lost things monsoon.

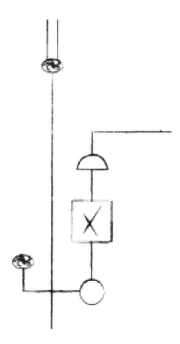

Detail: Laundry Room

Western Civ (Nymph Arethusa and **Quizlet's Crime Scene Search Methods**)

The sun was at my back. I saw a long shadow t**he entire scene is divided** stretching out before my feet, unless it was my fear that saw it, but certainly I feared the sound of feet, and the deep breaths **into zones** from his mouth stirred the ribbons in my hair. Weary with the effort to escape him, I cried out, "Help me, I will be taken. Diana, help the one **best for searching** who bore your weapons for you, whom you often gave your bow to carry, and your quiver with all its arrows!" The goddess was moved **for a small object**, and raising an impenetrable cloud, threw it over me.

g

o

h

our s

deep cuttings for the fastening of feet

wIth attached fIgures of mourners

The Team Compares Notes

what about instinct
someone said

what about
the things you want

CHAIN OF CUSTODY

DATE TIME	ITEM NO. QTY.	RELEASED BY: NAME, BADGE NO. SIGN	RECEIVED BY: NAME, BADGE NO. SIGN	REASON FOR CHANGE IN CUSTODY
1				
2				
3				
4				

boat-----boat
tight at the jetty
get lost   white rope

battleline

sideways-rushing sapphirine
where's Africa?

3 solo birds
in 8 hours

faultline

heat floats the wide-shouldered mountain

nothing's too much-she thinks (almost)---to bear

borderline

wind   window
whose language is this   tug

firing line

island, I've heard
　　　　the once-hated return
if you touch (please)
　　　　your stone lips to the sea

wrackline

----

what we remember

- →

what we want

bloodline

choose night (love's canopy)
           choose seeds from that tree
with the purple flowers

plumbline

boat
boatshadow
          (a throat kiss deep enough
          to reach all the colors)

the sharpest line may be the most
imaginary

it helps to know where you are
it helps

3
LIES DOWN WITH

primary transfer

direct contact between items from different aspects of the case or between victim and suspect after incident

secondary transfer

same person handling items from different aspects of the case

Quizlet's Crime Scene Search Methods

q. who wrote the book of fleeing?
        a. a pouch of fragments

q. what lies at a reasonable depth?
        a. the punctuating bone

\#

A woman lies down with a hawk.
She's climbed a camphor tree to rest in his wings.

Soon she twists in her sleep and they fall.
Now the hawk screams when women reach for him.

His shoulders, gripped once by earth, stay red.
But the woman's never slept so well.

How small that house looks from the treeline.
How beautiful the storm that takes it down.

q. why do caves descend and rivers gallop?
　　　　a. to absorb linearity

q. where is the terrace of what can be?
　　　　a. tally the children

#

A man lies down with a purple flower.
No one plans such passions.

Because the bloom needs so much water,
he sleeps with its stem in his mouth.

Not a soul notices how this dangler
hangs like an extra pajama sleeve

nor how his sweat slowly alters,
sweetening toward midnight.

q. what's the original dissonance?
       a. a nodding trigger

q. what waits in the fleshly mouth, open?
       a. excavation by angel

\#

A boy lies down with a rake.
The rake untangles his hair

(wild—he's a born thrasher).
Inch by inch the rake reverses

until it resembles a sharp third foot.
When the boy stumbles distraught

through time's bright fields,
the rake will be as quietly useful as ever.

q. what has been combed out of the body?
        a. the devil of day

q. what's the best part of a breeze?
        a. divulged afterwards

\#

A curtain lies down with a window.
Neither can see very well.

We'll be mysteries to each other,
they promise with flickering touches.

Shssh, a breeze wobbles.
That's what you think.

Valley mountain valley mountain
toils the ocean, further off.

q. what's the ambition of passages?

       a. to opera our fate

q. why incise the names of the victors?

       a. the river ascends

\#

A yellow skirt lies down with a vine.
It just happens like that

in the warm impermanence of late afternoon.
Maybe there's a school bus

or a nearby feral cat stand-off.
Each yawns past the first sweaty tickle of boredom.

I'll pinch you, one hisses.
I'll cover up what you've done, boasts the other.

q. why hurry a battered century?

    a. to relieve the pattern

q. in what lies the ultimate noun of the day?

    a. (technically) birds

#
A bird flies into himself.
For mating? For battle?

Drunk on loquats, he doesn't know window.
Nor when what drifts into a yellow skirt

drying below became his own feathers.
Why the sweet-studded earth would,

for him, reach up and stop.
If this too counts as migration.

.

q. what's another word for spatterdock?

    a. besotted form

q. what's another term for continuous grief?

    a. voluptuous arts

\#
The city lies down in wind
or wind lies down with a city.

Always this tussle as breeze gussets itself
through alleys or snaps along flags.

What constitutes body?
If the countryside's heart is a limestone grave,

dirtier and dirtier, city wind is an ear
all the lost things spit into.

q. what marks the ancient geometries?
      a. half dark, half fizzing out

q. who expects repair?
      a. another pissed-off cup

4
LET'S TRY THIS AGAIN: HOW DID YOU TRAVEL?

The ancient Greeks **a woman friend** witnessed **pointed at** many sinkholes, ponors, caves, **some 5-6 women at the party** and other natural orifices in the rocky ground. **Then she told me how** they had envisioned a vast subterranean Under-Earth--**each had been** penetrated **sexually** by networks of caverns and tunnels containing water and fire. By integrating their real-life observations of karstic waters **assaulted by some man** with their speculative **I don't think I've been** visions of a subterranean Underworld, the Greeks rationally concluded that **the same** interconnected conduits exist **since** under the ground and under the sea, even at long distances.

Take It All Down

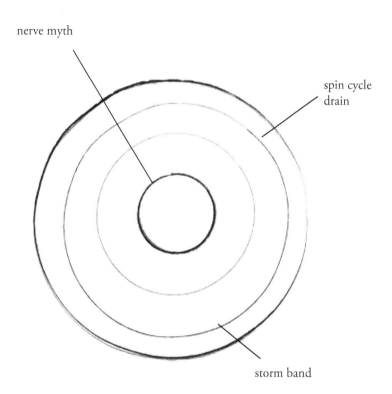

nerve myth

spin cycle
drain

storm band

Cry with one eye
(moon through rain).
EEEE says the eye chart.

Monks inhabiting the... **island**s claimed that one of the Springs originated on the ...mainland and then flowed through the seabed before emerging. The waters of this **island** spring were said to frequently contain objects that could have come only from the mainland. On one occasion, the spring fountain revealed a drinking cup fashioned from a gourd and adorned with silver.

Cindy Clendenon

Western Civ (Arethusa and **Museum Signage**)

Tired **implement** (I remember), I was returning from the woods. It was hot, and my
efforts had doubled the heat. I came to a river, without a ripple, hurrying on without
a murmur, clear to its bed, in whose depths you could count every pebble: you
would scarce think it moving **for removing**. Approaching, I dipped my toes in, then
as far as my knees, and not content with that I undressed, and draped my light
clothes on a hanging willow, and **foreign** plunged naked into the stream.
While I gathered the water **bodies** to me and splashed, gliding around in a thousand
ways, and stretching out my arms to shake the water from them, I thought **o** I heard
a murmur under the surface, and in fear I leapt for the **beautiful cup...**

Replace water with someone saying water.
Replace someone saying water with someone sleeping.
Replace someone sleeping with an empty glass.

Sex After Rape w/ Repurposed Landscape

The mirror refused her,
then the room.

Ok, she said.
I'll lie down in felled

laurel oak and chew grief's
pale herbage.

I'll take hooves.
A rule (the only one):

nothing understood
gets my love.

Bell, if you clang
that way, I'm not going.

deadline

In 2 minutes the door. In 5 minutes the blow. In 2 hours
the meeting. In 2 seconds that breath. Birds swoop, natter.
Try it again, landlubber. The distance from here to a treeline
by falling is what? The distance from me to you is 4 ropes
and what?

Western Civ   (Quizlet's Crime Scene Search Methods and **Arethusa's assailant** the river god Alpheus and **DONALD TRUMP**)

please wear clean disposable over-garments gloves and masks never talk over
he travelled I MOVED evidence clean all examination surfaces items should be
packed sealed and labeled **with her ON HER** before removal from the crime scene
through the seabed and not reopened before examination different police should deal
with different sides of the case **and resurfaced** victims and suspects should not
be transported **LIKE A BITCH** in the same car

Each time you drop something,
swallow your spit.

But Strategy 2 would end up being a radical development. It allowed the party-hat snails to squeeze water out of their bodies to produce a jet, whisking them away from predators. Eventually, **it took me about six months** the need for stronger muscles and faster movement resulted in the muscle **to go to my house** bulging out so much that it completely covered the shell. The it **almost** shell became internalized...**a** fossilized **year** funnel. Thus other strange ancient body plans **to spend the night** may still be found.

shard with human figure

in contiguous chambers

offering table with dolphins

variety of moveable finds

the weight of return not held in their bodies

clay lamp with erotic scene

multi-nozzled lamp

dentated tool

Pregnancy Test Strip

Is Someone Still Documenting This?

horn honking

laughs

sighs

chuckles

sighs

chuckles

sighs

clears throat

chuckles

clears throat

sniffles

chuckles softly

chuckles

voice breaking

sniffles

buzzer

buzzer

siren wailing

sighs

voice breaking

sighs

sighs

footsteps approach police radio chatter

sighs

horns honking

indistinct conversation

Card Handed to Officers Requesting Verbal Repetition

Do you have any diamond rings?

"   "

"   "

"   "

"   "

Card Handed to Officers Requesting Verbal Repetition

I think you're sexy
"   "

"   "

Disavow someone.
Disavow someone while standing in water.

The four boats were soon on the water; Ahab's in advance, and all **you know** swiftly pulling towards their prey. Soon it went down, and while, with oars suspended, we were awaiting its reappearance, lo! in the same spot **in my language** where it sank, once more it slowly rose. Almost forgetting **because of the ending** for the moment all thoughts of **the whale is** Moby Dick, we now gazed at the most wondrous phenomenon ......A vast pulpy mass, furlongs in length and breadth, of a glancing cream-colour, lay floating on the water....No perceptible face or front did it have; no conceivable token of either sensation or instinct; but undulated there on the billows **a girl**, an unearthly, formless, chance-like apparition of life.

w

a v e   s

e l e

g   y

why left In such small caves Is unknown

the length of a monster lifting a body

q. when is a document properly heroic?
      a. when it hides the washed parts separately

q. what is the first superstition of place?
      a. where the river convenes

A woman lies down at my door with a sponge.
Buzz. The door, crooked, stops halfway,

How long have I been loitering
in this shadow-stippled hall?

O seas, rise up.
She says the sponge will absorb any opening.

She says this will cost something
but not all I own.

I've got a fish in my **if we saw all things** tank who is swimming unbalanced. Its front half is up but the back half is like almost slanted down like a \ shape. All the other fish **that really surround us** are fine and the water levels of nitrates, ammonia, temp, etc. all seem like **we should be** normal. I don't have a...**unable** camera with me but I am going to see if I can find a video anywhere **to move** online. Here's the vid! Any advice!

History of the US (Christopher Columbus and **Shane MacGowan/ Sinead O'Connor**)

I looked over the whole of that **haunted** harbor and afterward returned to the ship and set sail and **by the ghost** I saw so many islands that I did not know how to decide which one I would go to first. And those **of your precious** men whom I had taken told me by signs that they were so very many that they were numberless. And they named by their **love** names more than a hundred.

A man lies down in rain.
This is not unusual

so let it pass
like rivers stealing the rusty edges of towns

or clouds torn sideways.
What is it about wishful thinking?

Blue! And see how he softens
though no one's touched him in years?

offline

"I can't think about that now," you say. "I just can't go there."

A land bird lies down in waves with a gull.
They aren't swimmers:

the gull tucks the smaller bird under his wing.
Next time a wave slides green over gold,

the bird's been flipped:
now the gull's beak rummages tiny white guts.

Forget about hunger. Forget about the next awful music.
That's it. Let go.

Detectives Work in Pairs

gulls crying GROANING SOFTLY zipper closes SHOWER RUNNING
BARKING IN DISTANCE sniffles SNIFFLES banging at door BANGING STOPS

out of line

There, there. If we ripple a finger over the screen, of course we can touch it. How hot it was. We climbed over the rope.

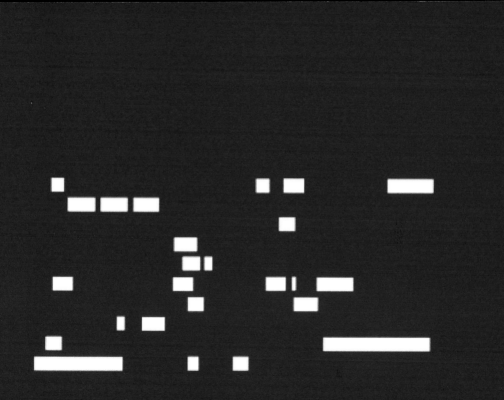

History of the US (Letter to Parole Board and Wobbly Screen)

As   who was raped and kidnapped from her   in   by John Wendell
Peltier   ,   ,   beg you not to release my assailant. As you know, Peltier
was convicted as a signature criminal—the rape of   is his signature as much as
the actual fingerprints on my   left when he vaulted back through without his
gloves for a second, horrifying   . The terror he induced (a loaded gun aimed at
my   ) the violation of my   (penetration in   , and   ), and the
threats he made (to kill not only   but my 3 sleeping   ) ARE his signature.
That's who he is.   No   should ever, ever, have to think he is out driving around
at   with his rape kit. Please don't release him—keep other
          safe from his   on my   .

FINAL DISPOSAL ACTION

RETURNED TO OWNER [ ]   DESTROYED [ ]   OTHER _____ DATE _____

OFFICER _____ SIGNATURE _____

NO. _____ OF _____ BAGS

CUT BELOW DOTTED LINE TO OPEN
. . . .

146

Before We Go, Can You Say Something Raped?

no

no

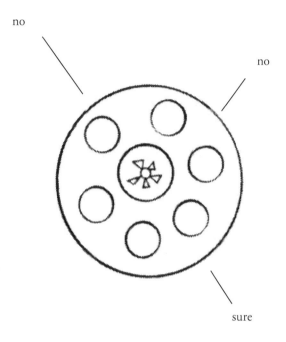

sure

Acknowledgements

Deepest thanks to the editors and curators who published, exhibited or otherwise included earlier versions in:

Versal, Barrow Street, Artborne, letterpress/smallportions (thanks for the beautiful chapbook), Saw Palm, Literary House Press, Poesial Visual

Oi, Futuro (Rio de Janeiro/Flamengo), which included animations by Dengke Chen of the layered/folded paper poems in Minotauoros, a solo show with Cyriaco Lopes, and published a selection of poems from The Rape Kit with translations into Portuguese by Cyriaco Lopes in their Poesia Visual series

Special thanks to curator Alberto Saraiva and his production team for this continuing collaboration

The Orlando Museum of Art, which included many of the q/a poems in Strangers, an augmented reality collaboration with Matt Roberts in the Florida Prize show in which Roberts was featured

Gallery at Avalon Island, which included 7 direction poems paired with images by Roberts in the annual Artborne show

Also:

Amandine Pras, Dengke Chen, and Matt Roberts, for a Brown Center grant-funded collaboration in instrument for removing foreign bodies, a multi-media performance including fragments from the book

Cyriaco Lopes for collaborative investigations of antiquities sites including Akrotiri and Volubilis (whose water system provides the crime scene/escape route map) and Ortygia (home of the spring of Arethusa) and the beautiful cover image

Amaranth Borsuk for an ongoing What's App collaboration which includes many of the water "directions"

Laura Mullen, Ronaldo Wilson, Jacklyn Gion and Carol Ann Moon for the Michael Jackson conversation at the first residency of Stetson University's MFA of the Americas which invited the History of the US poems

Disquiet International Literary Conference, which has allowed me to practice sections of the book as performance in Lisbon, Portugal

Ioannis Arhontakis for hosting a residency in Crete, and Thalia Trezos for the invitation

Art Sullivan and Melissa Sullivan, whose continued support of my work as the Sullivan Chair in Creative Writing at Stetson University has made the investigation of ancient sites possible

Many thanks to Daniel Quinn for the captchas

Thanks to Lucianna Chixaro Ramos for her work and help, especially in translating images— the fog machine is her own

Mark Jarman, who 31 years later took me back to the crime scene